For Rosa,
Jake and
Dali
M.L.

For Iris
and Rose
S.H.

First published in Great Britain in 2020 by Red Shed, an imprint of
Egmont Books UK a division of HarperCollins Publishers
1 London Bridge Street, London SE1 9GF
www.egmontbooks.co.uk

Text copyright © Matt Lucas 2020

Illustrations of Matt Lucas copyright © Matt Lucas 2020

Illustrated by Sarah Horne

All other illustrations copyright© Sarah Horne 2020

Matt Lucas and Sarah Horne have asserted their moral rights.

With special thanks to Rebecca Lewis-Oakes

ISBN 978 0 7555 0181 6

71494/004

Printed in Great Britain.

A CIP catalogue record for this book is available from the British Library.

# My Very Very Very Very Very Very Very SILLY BOOK of JOKES

# MATT LUCAS

## ILLUSTRATED BY SARAH HORNE

RED SHED

hello everybody i done a very very
very very very very very silly joke
book and i hope you like it jokes are
very special to me because sometimes
when i feel a bit sad i tell a silly joke
and then i feel at least halfway better
i think it is important to be silly i wish
more people would be silly and then
the world would be a better place or
at least a sillier one right lets get on
with the book we havent got all day
unless youve just woken up in which case
we have

# Hello, These Are the Contents

| | |
|---|---|
| Waiter, Waiter | 9 |
| Doctor, Doctor | 18 |
| Knock, Knock | 27 |
| Shaggy Dog Stories | 38 |
| What Do You Call ... | 57 |
| Jokes to Prove How Clever You Are | 69 |
| Punny Ha Ha | 78 |
| School's Out | 87 |
| Dad Jokes | 100 |
| Sporting Jokes | 108 |
| Old Jokes Home | 117 |
| *Your* Jokes | 127 |
| The Very Very Very Very Very Very *Very* Worst Jokes of All Time | 137 |

# Waiter, Waiter

and other ridiculously silly jokes involving food although theres no jokes involving cheese because i absolutely hate cheese eew it stinks no thank you i would far rather just eat choccie biccies but apparently you cant just eat choccie biccies you have to eat healthy food as well like lettuce honestly i might as well just be a rabbit

**Waiter, Waiter, do you serve lobster?**

Take a seat, Sir, we serve anybody

**Waiter, Waiter, is there soup on the menu?**

No, Madam, I wiped it off

**Waiter, Waiter, my plate's all wet**

That's the soup, Sir

**Waiter, Waiter, I have a fly in my soup!**

Keep it down, everyone will want one

apparently if you eat a fly by accident it will lay an egg inside you and then that fly will hatch and lay another egg and so on and one day you will have so many flies inside you that you will be able to hover six feet off the ground ha ha not really but it would be cool

**Waiter, Waiter, what's this fly doing in my soup?**

It looks like the backstroke, Sir

**Waiter, Waiter, bring me something to eat and make it snappy**

How about a crocodile sandwich?

**Waiter, Waiter, do you have frogs' legs?**

No, I've always walked like this

**Waiter, Waiter, there's a caterpillar in my salad**

Don't worry, there's no extra charge

## Waiter, Waiter, there's a small slug in my lettuce!

I'm terribly sorry, Madam, would you like me to get you a bigger one?

eew lettuce no thanks boring the slug probably tastes nicer

## What did the mayonnaise say to the fridge?

Close the door, I'm dressing!

## Why did the jelly wobble?

Because it saw the milkshake

**Waiter, Waiter, there's a black cat on my table!**

They're supposed to be lucky

**This one is, it's eating my lunch!**

**Waiter, Waiter, this egg is bad**

Don't blame me,
I only laid the table

**How do you make a sausage roll?**

Push it down a hill!

ha funny can you think of a word that rhymes with sausage i can possidge mum says its not an actual word but so what

14

**Waiter, Waiter, will my pizza be long?**

No, Madam, it will be round

**What do ghosts eat for tea?**

Scream cakes

**How do you know when there's an elephant in your fridge?**

Footprints in the butter

**How do you know when there are two elephants in your fridge?**

The door won't close

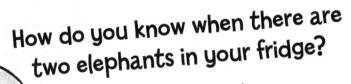

Waiter, Waiter, what's this cockroach doing in my ice-cream sundae?

Skiing, Sir

Waiter, Waiter, there's a fly in my soup

Don't worry, the spider on your bread will soon get it

Waiter, Waiter, what's this fly doing in the butter?

It must be a butterfly

did you know that butterflies go into a raccoon and turn into a caterpillar or something

Waiter, Waiter, please may I have the steak?

With pleasure, Madam

No, thank you! With chips, please

What did the duck say as he left the restaurant?

Put it on my bill, please

who are your favourite ducks mine are Daffy Donald and Mickey Mouse but i think he is a mouse

What do whales eat?

Fish and ships

# Doctor, Doctor

and some other jokes involving hospitals and nurses etc but nothing too sad because no one wants to hear a joke about someone getting really badly maimed so its mainly just jokes about people having a blister or runny poo again

**Doctor, Doctor, I feel like I'm turning into a pancake**

Oh, how waffle

**Doctor, Doctor, I keep thinking I'm a clock**

Stop winding me up

eRR...

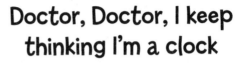

**Doctor, Doctor, I've got strawberries growing out of my head!**

I'll give you some cream for that

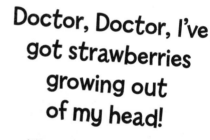

if you did have strawberries growing out of your head you would be delicious same with noodles but i think if you had a whole pizza growing out of your head that would just be weird

**Doctor, Doctor,
I keep thinking
I'm a bell**

Take these tablets
and give me a ring
in the morning!

**Doctor, Doctor, I keep getting
a pain in my eye when I drink coffee**

Have you tried taking the spoon out?

**Doctor, Doctor,
I've just swallowed a pen**

Well, sit down and
write your name

# Doctor, Doctor, I keep thinking I'm invisible

Who said that?

## A skeleton went into the doctor's office

The doctor said, 'Aren't you a little late?'

## An orange went to the doctor's: 'Doctor, Doctor, I just feel so tired all the time'

Doctor: 'I know what the problem is. You're out of juice'

orange is my favourite colour apart from blue and green and red and also yellow and purple

A patient walks into the surgery. The doctor says, 'Hello there, I haven't seen you in a while'

The patient says, 'No, I've not been very well . . .'

A banana went to the doctor's: 'Doctor, Doctor, I ache everywhere. Even my skin hurts'

Doctor: 'You're just not peeling very well'

Do you want to
hear a poo joke?

No, they
always stink

Doctor, Doctor, I think
I'm losing my memory

When did this start to happen?

When did what start to happen?

Doctor, Doctor,
I keep thinking I'm a dog

How long have you thought this?

Ever since I was a puppy

Doctor, Doctor,
I keep thinking I'm a dog

Take a seat

Oh, I'm not allowed on the furniture

24

# Where do you take a pony with a broken leg?

To the horsepital

# Doctor, Doctor, will this ointment clear up my spots?

I don't like to make rash promises

# Doctor, Doctor, I just got struck by lightning!

How do you feel?

**Shocking**

in cartoons it looks funny when someone is struck by lightning but i think in real life it could be quite annoying actually especially if you were holding a milkshake at the time and it made you drop your milkshake

DOCTOR

i like playing cards especially Top Trumps ive got football ones and superhero ones but they should do a Top Trumps of farts because farts are trumps ha ha

**Doctor, Doctor, I feel like a pack of cards**

I'll deal with you later

**Doctor, Doctor, everyone keeps ignoring me**

Next!

**Doctor, Doctor, I think I need glasses**

You certainly do. This is a fish and chip shop

**Doctor, Doctor, I'm not well. Can you help me out?**

Of course, which way did you come in?

my doctor told me i put on too much weight but he has a big jar of cookies in the waiting room so its his fault

# Knock, Knock

and other jokes involving doors if i can think of any but i havent managed any so far so i wouldnt get your hopes up

**Knock, knock**
Who's there?
**Luke**
Luke who?
**Luke through the keyhole
and you'll find out!**

**Knock, knock**
Who's there?
**Lena**
Lena who?
**Lena little closer and I'll tell you!**

**Knock, knock**
Who's there?
**Howl**
Howl who?
**Howl you know unless you
open the door?**

**Knock, knock**
Who's there?
**Avenue**
Avenue who?
**Avenue learned my name yet?**

**Knock, knock**
Who's there?
**Shirley**
Shirley who?
**Shirley you haven't forgotten my name already!**

my auntie shirley was a wonderful cook shes not dead she just cant be bothered to do it any more

**Knock, knock**
Who's there?
**Kam**
Kam who?
**Kam on in then!**

**Knock, knock**
Who's there?
**Norma**
Norma who?
**Normally I have a key . . .**

**Knock, knock**
Who's there?
**Yasin**
Yasin who?
**Yasin there's a bull on the loose?! Let me in!**

**Knock, knock**
Who's there?
**Alec**
Alec who?
**Alec the colour of your door!**

**Knock, knock**
Who's there?
**Ivor**
Ivor who?
**Ivor you open the door or I keep knocking**

**Knock, knock**
Who's there?
**Juicy**
Juicy who?
**Juicy my point**

juicy would be a good name especially if you were a actual orange but if you were a person then less so

**Knock, knock**
Who's there?
**Harry**
Harry who?
**Harry up and let me in!**

**Knock, knock**
Who's there?
**Emma**
Emma who?
**Emma bit cold out here, let me in!**

i like peas sometimes but other times i dont for instance they are nice with mashed potato but horrible in raspberry ripple ice cream

**Knock, knock**
Who's there?
**Peas**
Peas who?
**Peas let me in, it's really cold**

**Knock, knock**
Who's there?
**Lettuce**
Lettuce who?
**Lettuce in, it's freezing out here!**

**Knock, knock**
Who's there?
**Ash**
Ash who?
**Bless you!**
**I told you it was cold out here**

**Knock, knock**
Who's there?
**Howard**
Howard who?
**Howard you like to come out with me?**

for my birthday this year i am going bowling with some of my friends but the ball is quite heavy so i might just throw an egg down there instead ha ha

**Knock, knock**
Who's there?
**Abby**
Abby who?
**Abby birthday to you!**

**Knock, knock**
Who's there?
**Aunt**
Aunt who?
**Aunt you glad I'm here? I brought a cake**

33

**Knock, knock**
Who's there?
**Justin**
Justin who?
**Justin time to come in for tea**

**Knock, knock**
Who's there?
**Nadia**
Nadia who?
**Nadia head to the beat
of the music!**

do nod your head to the beat of the music if you like but dont nod it too much because you dont want it to fall off because it might land on your nose ouch

Knock, knock
Who's there?
**Noah**
Noah who?
**Noah good joke?**

In the bible
i think noah was the
one who built the ark
and put in two animals
i wonder why he
didnt make a bigger
ark and take more
with him

**Knock, knock**
Who's there?
**Aisha**
Aisha who?
**Aisha you won't
open that door?**

**Knock, knock**
Who's there?
**Yvonne**
Yvonne who?
**Yvonne you to
open the door**

**Knock, knock**
Who's there?
**Frank**
Frank who?
**Frank you very much for listening to my jokes!**

one of my old teachers was called frank so this really made me laugh ha ha oh no hang on he was called harvey my mistake

**Knock, knock**
Who's there?
**Boo**
Boo who?
**Don't cry, it's only a joke book!**

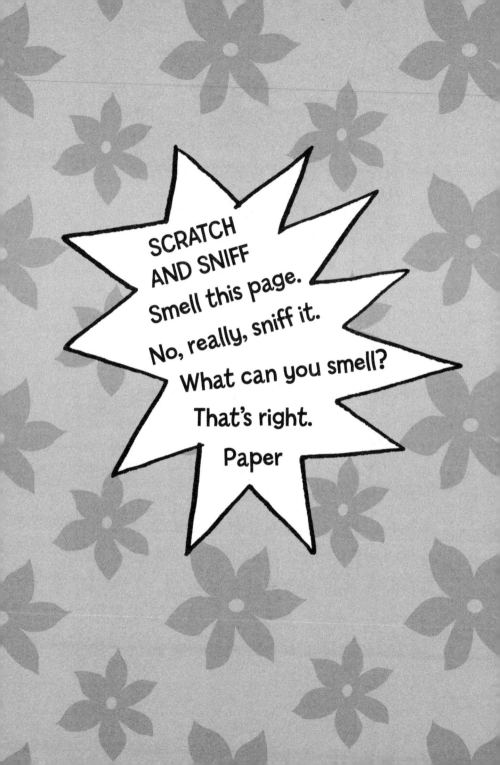

# Shaggy Dog Stories

by which i mean those jokes that are really really long rather than actual stories about shaggy dogs which would be probably quite boring i mean dogs are nice and that but they dont exactly have much to say ive certainly never had a good conversation with a labrador about Spongebob Squarepants for example

# The World's Greatest Comedian

Once upon a time there was a young girl called Rosa who wanted to become a comedian. She heard about the Greatest Comedian in the World, who lived on the top of a mountain. It was a very, very big and spiky mountain, covered in dangerous mountain attack-goats. The Greatest Comedian in the World was so funny that he had had to escape to this very-difficult-to-get-to mountain because he was hassled for jokes all the time. But legend had it that if someone could climb to the top of this very scary mountain, the Greatest Comedian in the World would tell them the secret to being very, very funny.

Rosa decided she needed the secret. She set out to climb the mountain.

She fell down. She got back up. She ran away

from the dangerous mountain attack-goats. They ran after her. She ran around their rocky pasture and then as they were still coming after her, she threw them some oat crackers and that stopped them long enough for her to climb further up the mountain.

Rosa had been on the mountain for what felt like years. She was on the verge of giving up.

But she didn't.

Eventually Rosa got to the top of the very, very big and spiky mountain, where she found the Greatest Comedian in the World.

The Greatest Comedian in the World said, 'Who the heck are you and why are you bothering me?'

Young Rosa panted – she was really out of breath because, as we just discussed, the mountain was, like, really big – and said, 'O Greatest Comedian in the World, I have come to learn the secret of being very, very funny.'

The Greatest Comedian in the World said, 'Ah, but I don't tell that to anyone! You have to climb a very, very big and spiky mountain and avoid my dangerous mountain attack-goats to be worthy of the secret.'

Rosa said, 'But I obviously have climbed the big and spiky mountain because, look, here I am.'

The Greatest Comedian in the World said, 'Oh, right, of course! Well, the secret to being very, very funny is . . .'

Wait, I'd tell you,
but YOU need to climb
the mountain first . . .

# The Insect Football World Cup

It was time for the Insect Football World Cup. Everyone was ready, except for the millipede, who had locked itself in the dressing room.

Everyone was very worried. They were wondering all kinds of things: is it too scared to come out? Does it have pre-match nerves?

The cockroach knocked on the door and asked if it wanted a cup of tea. No answer.

The wasp knocked on the door and asked if it wanted her to tell it a joke. No answer.

Finally, the team manager, the beetle, knocked on the door and said, 'You know, Millipede, me old pal, everyone gets nervous before a game. It's completely natural. What I do is—'

The millipede shouted back, 'Will you just WAIT?! I'm putting my boots on!'

maybe her name was millie pede too ha ha

44

# The Happily Married Couple

There was an old married couple who were very much in love. It was their golden wedding anniversary. That means they'd been married for, like, for ever. Their grandchildren asked them, 'How do you still get along so well after so many years, you very old people?'

The couple looked at each other and smiled. One of them said, 'Well, our secret is that every week we go to this gorgeous little restaurant. He orders lobster. I order steak. We always have the chocolate pudding. We cherish it so much.'

'Aw, what a lovely thing to do together,' said the grandchildren.

'Together? I go on Tuesdays, he goes on Thursdays!'

# Visit to an Art Gallery

A very important and powerful politician (I won't name him but he has terrible hair and a ridiculous tan and lives in America) was in an art gallery. He was very busy on his phone. So busy that he hired his own guide to go round the gallery. He thought he was very clever and wouldn't listen to anything the actually-very-clever art gallery guide had to say.

They stopped at the first painting, which was of some sunflowers in a vase and the very important politician looked up from his phone and said, 'Eurgh, that's dreadful.'

The guide said, 'Sir, that is a van Gogh. It is very beautiful.'

The important politician shrugged. 'Well, I think it's rubbish. I could have done it myself.'

They went into the next room and stopped at a second painting, which was of a little bridge over a garden pond with lots of lily pads. The important politician looked at the painting with one eye and his other eye still on his phone and said, 'Yawn! This one is so boring!'

The guide was horrified. He said, 'But that is a Monet!'

The very important politician said, 'Pfff!'

They came to a third room and stopped in front of a picture of a man. The very important politician said, 'Eew, that one is truly disgusting, what rubbish.'

The guide smiled and said, 'That, Sir, is a mirror.'

# The Cat Olympics

In the Cat Olympics Swimming Final there were three cats left.

There was an American cat called One Two Three, a French cat called Un Deux Trois, and a German cat called Eins Zwei Drei.

The German cat finished first, the American cat finished second, but the French cat was nowhere to be seen.

They looked everywhere, but sadly Un Deux Trois Quatre Cinq.

HEE HE HEEE!

# The Football Goalie

A small boy climbed a tall tree then found he couldn't get down. His cries for help were heard by a passing man.

'Just jump,' the man yelled. 'I'm a football goalie. I can catch you.'

The boy thought about it and decided he needed more information.

'Wait,' he said. 'What team do you play for?'

'Tottenham,' shouted the man.

'Ehhhh,' shrugged the boy. 'On second thoughts, I'm better off up here.'

# The Balloon Family

One day it was raining, so Mummy Balloon, Daddy Balloon and Baby Balloon were all watching telly indoors. Baby Balloon soon heard snoring – both her parents had dozed off on the sofa. Lazy balloon parents!

Baby Balloon knew the sofa was really comfy, so she went to sit on it too. But the sofa was too small. Baby Balloon tried to squeeze herself in but she couldn't.

I know, thought Baby Balloon, I'll just make a bit more room.

Very carefully and quietly, so as not to wake her parents, she untied Daddy Balloon's knot and let out a little air.

She still couldn't fit onto the sofa.

Very, very quietly, she untied Mummy Balloon's knot and let out a little bit of air.

Baby Balloon nearly fit but not quite!

So she untied her own knot and let out a little bit of air.

i wish i could make balloon animals the only balloon animal i can really do is a fat hamster which is just a balloon to be honest

Now she fitted easily on the sofa. It was so comfy that soon she was asleep too.

When she woke up, horror of horrors, her parents were awake and very angry! Daddy Balloon frowned at her and said, 'We are very upset about what you did. You let me down, you let your mother down, but worst of all, you let yourself down.'

# Bob's New Job

Bob was out of work. The button factory had closed down and he couldn't find an opening anywhere in town. He looked farther and farther away from home, until one day he stumbled across the zoo.

'Please, zookeeper,' said Bob. 'Have you got any jobs?'

The zookeeper looked up from her security cameras in the zookeeper hut and said, 'No.'

Bob turned around and started to walk out. He was so sad.

'Wait!' cried the zookeeper. 'All the monkeys seem to have run away. Could you dress up as a monkey for me?'

'I'd be delighted!' said Bob. So he put on the monkey suit and went into the monkey enclosure. He ate a lovely lunch of bananas.

But then he realised that the monkey enclosure was next to the lion enclosure. And there was a great big hole in the fence!

One of the lions was prowling around and noticed the hole too. It started walking over!

This is the end, thought Bob. 'Help, help!' he cried. 'The lion's coming to get me!'

But no one came. I forgot to mention, but it wasn't a very busy zoo. And the zookeeper was having a cup of tea instead of watching her security cameras.

Bob was desperate. 'Please don't eat me, lion!' he yelled. 'I'm a person, not a monkey! I'm just dressed up in a monkey suit. I am not tasty at all, I promise!'

'SHHHH!' said the lion. 'Keep your voice down or we'll all be out of a job.'

# A Frog Experiment

In a secret science lab, an evil scientist was doing a test on a frog. He told the frog to jump, so it jumped.

The evil scientist wrote down: *4 legs - jumps.*

Then the evil scientist cut off one of the frog's front legs and told it to jump. The frog jumped.

The evil scientist wrote down: *3 legs - jumps.*

Then the evil scientist cut off the other of the frog's front legs and told it to jump. The frog jumped.

The evil scientist wrote down: *2 legs - jumps.*

Then the evil scientist cut off one of the frog's back legs and told it to jump. The frog jumped.

The evil scientist wrote down: *1 leg - jumps.*

Then the evil scientist cut off the frog's last leg and told it to jump.

The frog did not jump.

The evil scientist wrote down: *no legs – goes deaf.*

What's the definition of a wild goose chase?

See page 86

# What Do You Call . . .

this is a chapter where all the jokes go what do you call and then theres something funny at the end of it well i think theyre funny and if you dont then maybe you should take this book back to the shop though if youre anything like me youve probably already lost the receipt so youre stuck with it you could use it to prop up a wobbly table i suppose or give it away to someone you dont like

What do you call
a bird with no eyes?

A brd

What do you call a boomerang
that won't come back?

A stick

Why are there four 'd's in the
name Edward Woodward?

Because otherwise he'd be
called Eewaa Woowaa

What do you call the
outside of a tree?

Bark

Woof, woof!

# What do you call a kangaroo eye doctor?

A hoptician

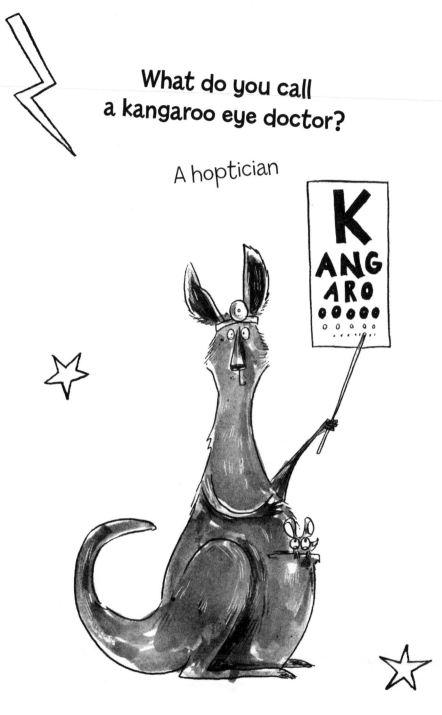

What do you call a man with a spade on his head?

Doug

What do you call a man without a spade on his head?

Douglas

What do you call a man with a seagull on his head?

Cliff

my mum loves to listen to this singer called cliff richard all the oldies love him hes like liam payne for people who are 104

What do you call a man
who walks all day?

Miles

i know someone
called miles but i dont
know anyone called
kilometres

What do you call a man
with a nose like a duck?

Bill

What do you call a boy
lying by the front door?

Matt

# What do you call a centipede crossed with a parrot?

A walkie-talkie

# What do you call a sleeping bull?

A bulldozer

# What do you call a monkey that floats in the air?

A baballoon

i really really want a pet monkey they are so funny but apparently it is not a good idea as they get really angry and throw their poo at you sometimes though if they do you could always throw yours back i suppose

i feel a bit sorry for pirates as there arent as many ships these days i wonder if they just steal canoes and pedalos now

**What do you call a pirate**

**who's always making mistakes?**

Wrong John Silver

**What do you call a very smelly fairy?**

Stinkerbell

# What do you call a boy with '9 out of 10' written on his face?

Mark

> my brother once drew Pac-Man on the back of my head in blue marker and it took three weeks to come out my mum was not happy but i didnt mind too much actually

# What do you call a girl with a tortoise on her head?

Shelley

# What do you call a girl with a frog on her head?

Lily

What do you call a girl with a storm on her head?

Gail

there is a woman in Coronation Street called gail ive never seen it but my mum likes it i prefer Scooby-Doo but not the ones with Scrappy-Doo in

What do you call a girl with
a reef on her head?

Coral

What do you call a girl who stands
between two goalposts?

Annette

What do you call a girl
with a boulder on her head?

Squashed

## What do you call a train loaded with toffee?

A chew-chew train

i got a train set for christmas once but it has a piece missing and so the train always falls off and then i make a noise of all the passengers grumbling and complaining its funny

## What do you call a plant growing out of your bottom?

Bum-boo

What do you call a bee that can't make up its mind?

A maybe

What do you call a man in a pile of leaves?

Russell

did you know there is a actor called russell crow so if you had a pet crow it would be funny if you called him russell although i dont think many people have a crow for a pet actually and russell budgerigar doesnt sound as good

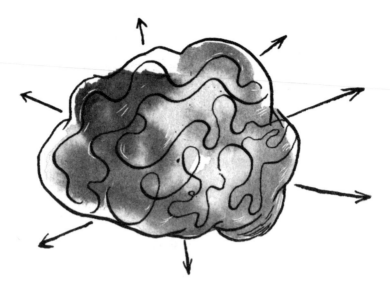

# Jokes to Prove How Clever You Are

these are the sort of jokes you can tell to annoy grown ups when they are telling you off for not tidying your room or for getting chocolate down your shirt so i like these kind of jokes because they trick people who think they are cleverer than you even though they probably actually are cleverer than you if im being honest

# What gets wet as it dries?

A towel

my mum always tells me off for leaving the bath towel on the floor but she should thank me because in a way i am cleaning the floor for her

# What's the difference between see and sea?

You can see the sea, but the sea cannot see you!

Pete and Repete were in a boat. Pete fell out. Who was left?

Repete.

Pete and Repete were in a boat. Pete fell out. Who was left?

Repete.

Pete and Repete were in a boat. Pete fell out. Who was left?

Repete.

repeat the joke until your friend gets really annoyed

# What do giraffes have that no other animal has?

Baby giraffes

i once saw a giraffe at the zoo he wasnt one of the exhibits he had bought a ticket like everybody else ha ha not really it would be funny though

# What's the first thing a Nobel Prize-winning scientist does in the morning?

Wakes up

# What do you get if you times 13 by 42, subtract 53 and divide by 6?

A headache

## What animal can jump higher than a house?

Any animal –
a house can't jump

## Give me a sentence starting with 'I'

I is—

## No, you must always say, 'I am . . .'

OK, I *am* the ninth letter of the alphabet

alphabet has 26 letters in it and also 8 ha ha

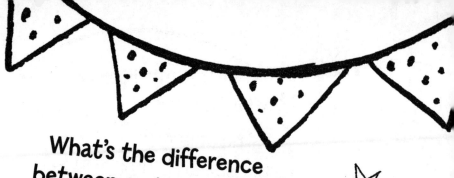

What's the difference between an iceberg and a clothes brush?

One crushes boats and the other brushes coats

What has a bottom at its top?

A leg

What's green and smells like blue paint?

Green paint

Why are ghosts bad liars?

You can see right through them

# MY VERY VERY VERY VERY

A TO Z BY ALF A. BET

How to Get Rich Quick by Robin Banks

Potty Training by Enid A. Wee

GREAT MYSTERIES BY HUGH DUNNIT

NEVER MAKE A MERMAID ANGRY BY SHEILA TACK

MAGIC SPELLS BY L. B. A. WITCH

A Load of Old Rubbish by Stefan Nonsense

# VERY VERY VERY SILLY LIBRARY:

HORRENDOUS HURRICANES BY RUFUS BLOWNOFF

THE WORST STRIKER BY MR GOAL

THE BIG BANG BY DINA MITE

CRIME DOES NOT PAY BY LORNA ORDER

# Punny Ha Ha

these are mostly jokes that involve words that sound the same but are spelled differently i actually find these kind of jokes quite annoying but i need to fill this book up otherwise therell be loads of empty pages and then youll get shirty with me and youll want your money back which i cant do because ive already spent it on a Cornetto

**Why was the beach wet?**

Because the seaweed

**How is the sea held in place?**

Its tide

wouldnt it be good if you could actually move the sea somewhere a bit nearer to where you live i would move it to the end of my street i wouldnt move it any nearer because i wouldnt want my dinner to get soggy

**What do you get when you cross an elephant with a fish?**

Swimming trunks

# Which fruit is never by itself?

A pear

## Did you hear about the piano player who kept banging their head against the keys?

They were playing by ear

i cant play the piano but i am pretty good at the kazoo im like the justin bieber of the kazoo in fact though he is rubbish

## How do you make a bandstand?

Take away their chairs

How do you get a baby astronaut to sleep?

Rocket

Why did the wheel stop rolling?

It was tyred

When do astronauts eat?

At launch time

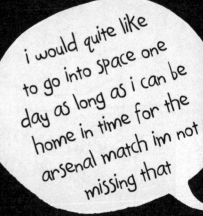

What's brown and sticky?

A stick

**Why did the computer squeak?**

Somebody stepped on its mouse

**Why do bees have sticky hair?**

Because they use honeycombs

**Where do you weigh a whale?**

At the whale-weigh station

i wonder how many whales there are in wales i imagine there must be at least one and if he doesnt like it there i bet he wails ha ha

Did you hear about the dancer who fell through the floor?

It was just a stage he was going through

i once fell off the floor but nobody believes me but i did

What do you do if you split your sides laughing?

Run till you get a stitch

What does a cloud wear under her coat?

Thunderwear

# Why does Peter Pan always fly?

Because he can Neverland!

peter pan is known as the boy who never grew up and also so am i because every time i am naughty my mum tells me to grow up and she has been telling me that for years and i still havent

## Where do sheep get their hair cut?

At the baa-baa's

## Why do you find toadstools so close together in the forest?

They don't need mushroom

i dont like mushrooms but i do like mushrooms on toast no i cant explain it either

# What's the definition of a wild goose chase?

See page 56

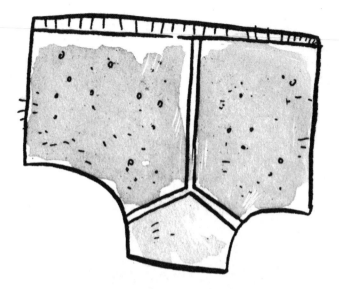

# School's Out

these are jokes about school do you know whats
weird even though i left school years ago and
am now an actual grown up with my own house
and a job i still have nightmares about being
back at school in my underpants whats that
all about

# What do you do if your teacher rolls her eyes at you?

Pick them up off the floor and roll them right back!

my teacher always told me off for rolling my eyes so i now just cross them instead

# How many children can you fit into an empty classroom?

One - after that, it's not empty!

# What's a witch's favourite subject?

Spelling

eRR...?

$25 \times 200,000 = ?$

$17 + 17 = ?$

## What do elves do after school?

Gnomework

## How do bees get to school?

On the school buzz

i hate doing homework i would have asked my grandad to go and do it for me but i was worried in case his false teeth fell into my lunch box

**Why is 6 afraid of 7?**

Because 7 8 9

if you are reading this joke to someone dont say why is six afraid of seven because seven hundred and eighty nine because everybody will just think you are nuts

**Why did the music teacher need a ladder?**

To reach the high notes

What did the choir send their music teacher when she was sick?

A get-well-soon chord

Why was the music teacher arrested?

She was in treble

our music teacher is always teaching us hymns but never hers ha ha

# When are school uniforms fire hazards?

When they're blazers

not gonna lie i loved it when the fire alarm went off in school if it meant getting out of maths but once it went off while i was at the front of the tuck shop queue and i was livid i bought some Rolos on the way home but it wasnt the same

**Miss, would you punish someone for something they haven't done?**

Never!

**Excellent. I haven't done my homework**

**Pupil: I'm sad. Today I learned that words can be hurtful**

Teacher: Oh no, are you being bullied?

**Pupil: No, I dropped a dictionary on my foot**

**Have you ever had problems with algebraic formulas?**

Only when I try to spell it

i wonder if women maths teachers wear algebras ha ha

i like cake but i dont like fish cake imagine getting a fish cake for your birthday cake yuck it would be funny though

**Pupil: Miss, I can't hand my homework in**

Teacher: Why not?

**Pupil: Because I ate it**

Teacher: Why on earth did you eat your homework?

**Pupil: Because you said it was a piece of cake**

**Miss, Miss, sorry we're late for class, the school bus got a puncture!**

Oh no, what happened?

**There was a fork in the road**

**Teacher: Why have you drawn a wooden desk for this experiment?**

Pupil: You told us to draw what we could see under the microscope

**My teacher and I just couldn't agree I said: Look, I'll meet you halfway – I'll admit you're wrong if you admit I'm right**

**How do you know there's been a snowman in the classroom?**

It's wet

## My teacher asked me:
## How do you spell 'cucaracha'?

I said: K-O-O-K-A-A-R-A-C-H-A-H

### He said: That's not how the dictionary spells it

I said: You didn't ask me how the dictionary spells it

it is true though and when you ask a teacher how to spell a word and they say look it up in the dictionary how are you supposed to look it up in the dictionary if you dont know how it is spelled in the first place honestly sometimes grown ups are an idiot

# Dad Jokes

these are jokes about parents and also the sort of annoying jokes that dads tell that make them laugh their heads off and make everyone else go thats about as funny as fart in a spacesuit actually come to think of it if you did fart in a spacesuit it wouldnt be that bad because your own ones are never as rotten as someones elses i dont know why

**Dad, I've got this teapot for Granny**

What a great swap

**What do you call a dad with a banana in each ear?**

Anything you like, he can't hear you!

**Dad, you're walking funny. Do you have holes in your pants?**

Certainly not!

**Then how do you get your legs through?**

did you know in america they call trousers pants they also call the pavement the sidewalk but they call pillows pillows like we do

**What did the baby volcano say to the daddy volcano?**

I lava you

**What time is it when an elephant sits on your fence?**

Time to get a new fence

if an elephant sits on your fence it is probably your own fault for inviting her to your barbecue mind you she would be able to put the fire out nicely at the end with her trunk so its not a bad idea actually

What do you call a snowman in August?

A puddle

What did one eye say to the other?

Between you and me, something smells

What do magnets say to each other on Valentine's Day?

I find you very attractive

HEE HE HEEE!

What's the hardest thing about skydiving?

The ground

If you have three apples in one hand and five apples in the other hand, what do you have?

Massive hands

# Where do you find giant snails?

On the ends of giants' fingers!

# Why is Sunday stronger than Thursday?

Because Thursday is a weak day

## How many dancers does it take to change a lightbulb?

Five, six, seven, eight . . .

## Why do dogs run in circles?

It's hard to run in squares

Sometimes my mum tells me off for eating like a dog but when my dog eats like a dog my mums says well done it makes no sense

## How do you make monkey toast?

Under the gorilla

# What do you get if you sit under a cow?

A pat on the head

apparently animal poo makes the grass grow but i dont believe it because if it was true surely grass would be brown wouldnt it

## What do ghosts call their mum and dad?

Transparents

## Why do birds fly south in the winter?

Because it's too far to walk

What has eight legs, six eyes, a hairy back and a poisonous tail?

I don't know

Well, there's one on your back right now!

i would like eight legs and then i could play in goal for arsenal and also it would be much easier to scratch my back probably

**Fifteen toilets have been stolen in the local village**

The police have nothing to go on

# Sporting Jokes

these are jokes about
sports which is perfectly flippin
obvious if you ask me
are you a nitwit

## Why did the footballers get cold?

The stadium was packed with fans

## One football said to another, 'Wow, the strikers are dreadful this year'

The other football said, 'Argh! A talking football!'

thinking about it if a football could actually speak it would probably say ow a lot and maybe it would even kick you back so be careful

**Where do frogs get changed for football?**

In the croakroom

**Why is Cinderella no good at footie?**

Because she's always running away from the ball

i saw a cartoon of cinderella once it was good it had a song in it that goes bibiddi bobbidi boo and my mum said they are not real words but they are she just obviously hasnt seen the film

**Did you hear about the two vampires in the 100 metre sprint final?**

Yes, it was neck and neck

What bird is always
out of breath at
the end of a race?

A puffin

What do Arsenal players
have in common with
magicians?

They both love hat tricks

111

# Why did the sprinter run round his bed?

He wanted to catch up on his sleep

i cannot run round my bed because it is up against the wall i could move it i suppose the bed not the wall ha ha

# What sport are waiters really good at?

Tennis, because they serve so well

# Why are fish rubbish at tennis?

They don't like getting
too close to the net

have you noticed that every year when
wimbledon is on everyone suddenly loves
tennis and plays it nonstop in their garden
for two weeks and then forgets about it
again straight away

Two football teams play and the
home team wins. But not a single
man from either team scores
a goal. How can this be?

They were women's
teams, obviously!

## How do zebras play baseball?

Three stripes and you're out

## Why are babies good at basketball?

They're always dribbling

actually if babies did play basketball it would be hard because they cant even stand up you could call it basketcrawl instead i suppose ha ha

## Why did the golfer wear two pairs of pants?

In case he got a hole in one

## What lights up a football stadium?

A football match

## Why should you never play sport in the jungle?

Because there's always a cheetah

also you shouldnt play sport in the jungle because a monkey might go into your bag while you are playing and steal your Capri-Sun i seen something like this on YouTube monkeys are naughty

**I watched ice hockey before it was cool**

Oh no, hang on, it was swimming. I watched swimming

HEE HE HEEE!

**Which is the warmest athlete?**

The long jumper

# Old Jokes Home

these are jokes set in the olden days like robin hood or dick turpin and if youre not sure who these kind of people are then you should start listening in history lessons instead of nattering to the person next to you about jadon sancho and picking your nose and eating it eew bogies are disgusting but also strangely delicious but no one ever admits that do they

## Where do you find Hadrian's Wall?

At the bottom of Hadrian's garden

## Which fruit launched a thousand ships?

Melon of Troy

## When did Queen Victoria die?

A few days before they buried her

queen victoria was the queen in victorian times what a coincidence that she was called victoria

## Where are the kings and queens of England usually crowned?

On their heads

# When did nerds rule the earth?

The Dork Ages

**King Arthur had a terrible dream that Sir Lancelot tried to chop off his head!**

It was a knightmare

**Why is 476 to 1453ce called the Dark Ages?**

Because there were so many knights

actually i think it was called the dark ages because it was a long time ago and lightbulbs didnt exist yet and so people couldnt see much

119

How did Vikings send
secret messages?

Norse code

What did Vikings call
English villages?

Chopping centres

Where did General
Custard die?

At the Battle of
Little Cream Horn

Where do baby
Vikings sleep?

In the Norsery

How do you use an ancient
Egyptian doorbell?

Toot and come in

**What do Alexander the Great and Kermit the Frog have in common?**

Their middle names

**What did the pharaoh say when he saw the pyramids?**

Mummy's home!

i never saw the film of The Mummy but i did go on The Mummy ride at Universal Studios so i feel like i have

**What's a mummy's favourite music?**

Wrap

**Who designed Noah's ark?**

An ark-itect

121

**What's the worst thing about Ancient History in school?**

The teacher tends to Babylon

our history teacher at school was so old we used to say he was just telling us his memories ha ha

**Who was the librarian on Bluebeard's pirate ship?**

Captain Book

**How was the Roman Empire cut in half?**

With a pair of Caesars

**Why did Romans build straight roads?**

So their armies didn't go round the bend

**What does the Statue of Liberty stand for?**

She can't sit down

**Why did Captain Cook sail to Australia?**

It was too far to swim

because australia is the other side of the world if you swam there when you arrived you would be swimming upside down with all the water on top of you and the sky underneath you ha ha not really

**Where did Henry VIII keep his armies?**

Up his sleevies

## Queen Elizabeth I only played cards on the toilet

She was guaranteed a royal flush

when you see paintings of queen elizabeth the first she has really black teeth she should have used toothpaste but it wasnt invented yet but she could still have had a Smint then

**When was Rome built?**

At night

**What makes you think that?**

I've heard that Rome wasn't built in a day

**What did Julius Caesar say when Brutus stabbed him?**

'Ouch!'

HEE HE HEEE!

**Why did King Tutankhamun fail his exams?**

He didn't finish his cursework

**What is written on the outside of Rameses' pyramid?**

'Tomb it may concern . . .'

## What did ancient Gauls inscribe their records on?

Gaulstones

## Viking warriors were not afraid of death

They knew they'd be Bjorn again

## Who stole from the rich to pay for the bows in his hair?

Ribbon Hood

Somebody told me that julius caesar ate two brute i dont know what brute are but they must be pretty tasty if he ate two of them

## Caesar: What's the weather today?

Brutus: Hail, Caesar

FFFFTT!

# Your Jokes

these are jokes that have been sent in by
readers some of them make no sense at all
and actually these ones made me laugh even
more i dont know why

**What do you call a unicorn that has done a poo?**

A poonicorn!
Iris, age 6

**What did the policeman say when he looked under his shirt?**

Freeze! You're under a vest
Grace, age 8

**Where do birds put their rubbish?**

In the ro-bin
Harry, age 4

do you know there was a robin in my garden last week he was looking for Batman ha ha not really

**What do you call two robbers?**

A pair of knickers
Jamie M, age 7

Knock, knock
Who's there?
**The interrupting cow**
The interrupt—
**MOO!**
Jamie L, age 6

**What does a frog say when you offer it a book?**

Reddit,
reddit,
reddit
Becky, age 4

maybe when you have finished with this book you could give it to a frog she might like to read it while she is eating her toad in the hole ha ha

**What do you call a sleeping dinosaur?**

A dino-snore-us
Asha, age 9

**What did the rug say to the floor?**

I've got you covered
Jeffrey, age 7

# What do you call a one-eyed dinosaur?

A do-you-think-he-saw-us?

*Steve, age 10*

# What do you call a magic dog?

A Labracadabrador

*Joshua, age 5*

# I made a ventriloquist's dummy out of old bits of carpet

It was ruggish

*Grant, age 53*

grant is 53 he is not even a child he should not be in this bit if you see him tell him to go home

## Why did the hippopotamus tell a joke?

Because his dad forced him to
*Seb, age 7*

you never see a hippo smile but if you did you could call it a happyPotamus
ha ha

## What do you say to an ape who calls you on the phone?

Who-rang-utang?
*Rose, age 9 months*
*(with help from her mum and dad)*

## How do you cheer up a baked potato?

You butter him up
*Asha, age 9*

i done a song about a baked potato sometimes people get cross with me because it goes round and round in their head and they cant sleep
ha ha

**What do you do if you're stuck inside an elephant?**

Run around till you're all pooped out
*Nicole, age 4*

**What smells like a tomato but you can't see it?**

A tomato trump
*Agatha, age 4*

**What monkey is not yours?**

A notyomonkey
*Agatha, age 4*

Potato rhymes with tomato unless you say it

**What is a leaf called if it's on a tree?**

A leaf leaf
*Agatha, age 4*

this is my favouritest joke of all

**Why were the baker's hands brown?**

Because he kneaded a poo!
*Sioned, age 6*

**What's orange and sounds like a parrot?**

A carrot
*Katie, age 6*

**What do you call an elephant with a potato?**

Mashed potato
*Amina, age 6*

**Who shouted 'knickers' at the Big Bad Wolf?**

Little Rude Riding Hood
*Isobel, age 6*

133

**Why was the potato such a meanie in the playground?**

Because it wasn't a sweet potato!
*Asha, age 9*

**What kind of music do balloons NOT like?**

Pop music
*Catrin, age 3*

this might be true and maybe they eat raisins in the bath because they are wrinkly too

**Are old people wrinkly because they've been in the bath for too long?**
*Sioned, age 6*

**Knock, knock**
Who's there?
**WhatsApp**
WhatsApp who?
**What's A POO!**
*Emilia and Alice, ages 9 and 6*

**Why does Mr Tall have long legs?**

Because he has smelly feet!
*Madeleine, age 3 ½*

**Knock, knock**
Who's there
**Andy**
Andy who
**Andy bum**
*Rose D, age 3*

**Knock, knock**
Who's there?
**Europe**
Europe who?
**No, YOU'RE a poo!**
*Callum, age 7*

# How do you make an octopus laugh?

Ten tickles
*Chloe, age 5*

**Knock, knock**
Who's there?
**Banana**
Banana who?
**Knock, knock**
Who's there?
**Banana**
Banana who?
**Knock, knock**
Who's there?
**Banana**
Banana who?
**Knock, knock**
Who's there?
**Orange**
Orange who?
**Orange you glad
I didn't say banana!**
*Jack, age 6*

# What were the head lice doing at the craft competition?

Knitting
*Nina, age 6*

# What do monkeys train for?

Championchimps!
*Carys, age 7*

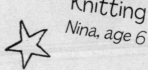

The
Very
Very
Very
Very
Very
*Very*
Worst Jokes
of All Time

# Honestly, these jokes are PANTS!

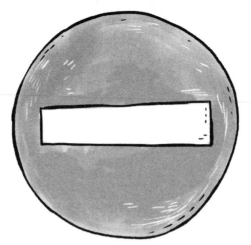

# The Very Very Very Very Very Very Very Worst Jokes of All Time

these are terrible do not read them go and do something else instead like watch tv but dont watch the news because i watched it once and it was just full of old people droning on i would much rather watch cartoons but not Peppa Pig because thats for babies i much prefer Pingu

## Why did the chicken cross the road?

To get to the other side

## Why did the cow cross the road?

To get to the udder side

## Why did the dancer cross the road?

They had to do it on the other side

there is this tv show called Strictly where all these people do dancing i dont watch it its boring its good when they fall over though

**Why did the chicken cross the playground?**

To get to the other slide

**Why did the turkey cross the road?**

It was the chicken's day off

i went to turkey on holiday once but i didnt see any turkeys there just people what a con ha ha

**Why did the chicken cross the sea?**

To get to the other tide

**Why did the dinosaur cross the road?**

Because the chicken hadn't evolved yet

**Why is it so hard to tell jokes to a snake?**

Because you can't pull its leg

i once saw a snake in my cupboard and i was scared but it was just a belt but sometimes i pretend it is actually a snake and now i am too scared to open the cupboard door i am a idiot

# Why are cats rubbish at telling jokes?

They always fur-get the punchline

eRMM...

# Animal jokes?

Toucan play at that game

# We don't have many vegetable jokes yet

If you think of one, lettuce know

Did you hear the joke about the roof?

Never mind, it's over your head

A T. rex went into the doctor's with a terrible blister

It was a dino-sore

What's louder than an angry monster?

Two angry monsters

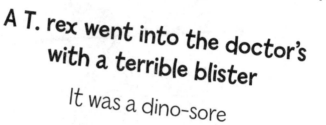

if i saw two angry monsters i would shrink myself and hide in a teacup but i hope nobody would drink me by accident

**What goes, 'Ha ha, plop'?**

Someone laughing their head off

**What do you call a joke book for chickens?**

A yolk book

149

Why do elephants paint themselves yellow?

So they can hide upside-down in the custard

Have you ever seen an elephant hiding upside-down in the custard?

No? Well, it must work then

custard is nice but sometimes it can burn your tongue so when you go to the supermarket make sure you buy a packet that is not too hot

What do you call a French man wearing sandals?

Filipe Folope

Have you heard the joke about the dustbin lorry?

It's a load of rubbish

What goes, 'Now you see me, now you don't, now you see me, now you don't'?

A talking penguin on a zebra crossing

i seen a zebra at a safari park and i really wanted to get a pen and colour in the rest of her ha ha but i didnt of course

What did the teddy bear say when he was offered pudding?

No, thanks, I'm stuffed

my teddy bear has no clothes on he is a bare bear ha ha

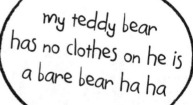

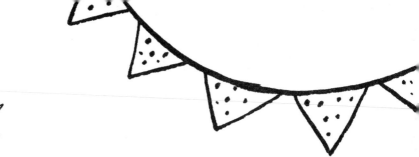

**What's the difference between this joke book and a postbox?**

If you don't know, I'm not sending you to post my letters!

**What's the difference between a joke book and a biscuit?**

You can't dunk a joke book in your tea

ok that is the end of the book thank you for reading it i would stay and tell you more jokes but i need to do a poo now bye

# Matt Lucas

MATT LUCAS is an actor, writer, comedian and very silly person. He became famous by playing a big baby who played the drums in a crazy TV show called *Shooting Stars*. His next TV show after that was called *Little Britain*, which he did with David Walliams. *Little Britain* was very rude indeed and you are not allowed to watch it until you are at least 75 years old.

Matt has played lots of other characters on TV, including Mr Toad in *The Wind in the Willows*, Bottom in *A Midsummer Night's Dream* (ha ha, I just said bottom) and the companion Nardole in *Doctor Who*, although it was too scary for Matt to watch. He has also appeared in lots of Hollywood films, such as *Paddington*, in which he played a cheeky London cabbie, and *Alice in Wonderland*, where he played Tweedle Dee and his equally silly brother, Tweedle Dum. Matt has also done voices for several cartoons, including Benny in *Gnomeo and Juliet*.

In spring 2020, Matt wrote and recorded a new version of his song *Thank You, Baked Potato* to raise money for FeedNHS. It went to the top of the download charts and Matt sang the song with lot of celebrities, including Brian May, Gary Barlow and the cast of *Coronation Street*.

Matt is also a radio presenter, an Arsenal supporter, and co-host of *The Great British Bake Off*, which is his dream job as he loves cake (but not cheesecake).

# Sarah Horne

SARAH HORNE is an illustrator, writer and music fan - especially the music of Bob Dylan and Fleetwood Mac. (Never heard of them? Ask your parents!) She first learned to draw aged nine, when she needed to explain to the hairdresser how she wanted her hair to be cut. The result was not what she had hoped for - but her picture was pretty amazing, even if she says so herself.

Since aged nine, Sarah's drawing has got better and better (and so have her haircuts). She has illustrated over 70 books, including *Charlie Changes into a Chicken*, *Fizzlebert Stump: The Boy Who Ran Away From the Circus (and joined the library)*, *Puppy Academy*, and *Ask Oscar* and its sequels. Most of the books she has drawn have been very, very silly.

Sarah's favourite things to draw are craggy faces and strange animals. She has never liked drawing bicycles or monkeys. Writing and illustrating books for children is pretty much Sarah's dream job, but if she could, she would also like to be a space scientist or musician, playing the trumpet or the drums. But as she doesn't have the skills for any of this yet, she's going to stick to drawing fun things.